MEXICO

R.L. Van

Big Buddy Books
An Imprint of Abdo Publishing
abdobooks.com

abdobooks.com

Published by Abdo Publishing, a division of ABDO, PO Box 398166, Minneapolis, Minnesota 55439.

Printed in the United States of America, North Mankato, Minnesota
102022
012023

Design: Emily O'Malley, Mighty Media, Inc.
Production: Mighty Media, Inc.
Editor: Jessica Rusick
Cover Photograph: Iryna Kalamurza/Shutterstock Images
Interior Photographs: AGCuest/Shutterstock Images, p. 30 (currency); Aleksandar Todorovic/Shutterstock Images, p. 26 (right); anarociogf/Shutterstock Images, p. 17; AndreyO/Shutterstock Images, p. 7 (map); biggereye/Shutterstock Images, p. 19; Ckn8u/Wikimedia Commons, p. 28 (top); Everett Collection/Shutterstock Images, pp. 11, 29 (top); Iryna Kalamurza/Shutterstock Images, pp. 26 (left), 28 (bottom); javarman/Shutterstock Images, p. 13; jejim/Shutterstock Images, p. 29 (bottom); Kobby Dagan/Shutterstock Images, p. 27 (top left); Luis Alberto Sanchez/Shutterstock Images, p. 23; Luis Alvarado Alvarado/Shutterstock Images, p. 6 (middle); lukulo/iStockphoto, pp. 5 (compass), 7 (compass); Magi Bagi/Shutterstock Images, p. 30 (flag); Monica Garza 73/Shutterstock Images, p. 6 (bottom); nyker/Shutterstock Images, p. 25; Patryk Kosmider/Shutterstock Images, p. 15; petegog/Shutterstock Images, p. 27 (top right); Pyty/Shutterstock Images, p. 5 (map); Simon Dannhauer/Shutterstock Images, p. 27 (bottom); Vadim Petrakov/Shutterstock Images, p. 9; Wikimedia Commons, p. 21; WitR/Shutterstock Images, p. 6 (top)
Design Elements: Mighty Media, Inc.
Country population and area figures taken from the CIA World Factbook

Library of Congress Control Number: 2022940513

Publisher's Cataloging-in-Publication Data
Names: Van, R.L., author.
Title: Mexico / by R.L. Van
Description: Minneapolis, Minnesota : Abdo Publishing, 2023 | Series: Countries | Includes online resources and index.
Identifiers: ISBN 9781532199684 (lib. bdg.) | ISBN 9781098274887 (ebook)
Subjects: LCSH: Mexico--Juvenile literature. | North America--Juvenile literature. | Latin America--Juvenile literature. | Mexico--History--Juvenile literature.
Classification: DDC 972.5--dc23

CONTENTS

1

PASSPORT TO MEXICO

Mexico is a country in North America. Three countries, the Pacific Ocean, the Gulf of Mexico, and the Caribbean Sea border it. About 129 million people live there.

DID YOU KNOW?

Mexico has 31 states and a federal district.

WHERE IS MEXICO?

IMPORTANT CITIES

Mexico City is Mexico's **capital** and largest **metropolitan area**. It is known for its history, businesses, and culture.

Guadalajara is Mexico's second-largest metropolitan area. It is a center of technology, finance, and culture.

Monterrey is Mexico's third-largest metropolitan area. It is known for business and manufacturing.

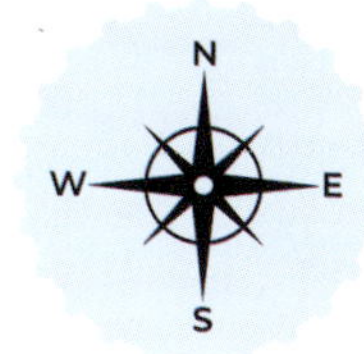

Monterrey
Population: 5.04 million

SAY IT

Mexico City
MEHK-sik-oh SIH-tee

Guadalajara
gwah-dah-lah-HAHR-ah

Monterrey
mahn-tuhr-AY

MEXICO

Guadalajara
Population: 5.34 million

DID YOU KNOW?

Mexico City is the oldest **capital** in the Americas and the most populous city in North America.

Mexico City
Population: 22.09 million

MEXICO IN HISTORY

The first people to live in Mexico were hunters. They followed animals there about 10,000 years ago. Over time, great **civilizations** formed. The Maya held power between 250 and 900. Beginning in the 1300s, the Aztecs built a civilization. The Spanish **conquered** them in the 1520s.

Teotihuacán is an ancient city in Mexico. Archaeologists are unsure which civilization built it.

Mexico declared independence from Spain in 1810. It won freedom in 1821. In the 1840s, Mexico and the United States fought over land.

The Mexican **Revolution** began in 1910. People fought to change Mexico's government. Today, Mexico struggles with poverty and crime. But people work to improve the country.

DID YOU KNOW?

Mexico honors Independence Day on September 16.

The Mexican-American War was fought from 1846 to 1848. Mexico lost nearly one-third of its land in the struggle.

AN IMPORTANT SYMBOL

Mexico's flag is green, white, and red. The Mexican emblem is in the center. It shows an eagle on a cactus eating a snake.

Mexico is a **federal presidential republic**. Congress makes laws. The president is head of state and government.

The Mexican emblem is inspired by a legend about the founding of the Aztec capital city.

ACROSS THE LAND

Mexico has deserts, coasts, forests, and rain forests. The Sierra Madre mountain range covers much of Mexico. The Rio Grande river forms Mexico's northern border.

Lizards, snakes, parrots, and fish live in Mexico. Evergreen trees, palm trees, cacti, and flowers grow there.

Between 10 and 12 percent of the world's plants and animals are found in Mexico.

EARNING A LIVING

Many Mexicans work in factories making cars and steel. Others have service jobs, such as teaching.

Mexico's **natural resources** include silver, gold, natural gas, and oil. Farmers grow corn, coffee, grains, and avocados. They also raise cattle.

Mexico exported more than $3 billion worth of avocados in 2021.

LIFE IN MEXICO

Popular foods in Mexico include beans, avocados, rice, and peppers. Fruity drinks and sweet breads are favorite treats. Soccer and baseball are popular sports.

Most Mexican people are Roman Catholic. Many people follow both Indigenous beliefs and Roman Catholic **traditions**.

Elote, or grilled corn on the cob, is a popular Mexican street food.

FAMOUS FACES

Frida Kahlo was born in Coyoacán, Mexico, in 1907. She began painting after a serious accident at age 18. Kahlo painted about her experiences, her heritage, and society. She was the first 20th-century Mexican artist featured in the Louvre Museum in France. Kahlo died in 1954.

Frida Kahlo was known especially for painting self-portraits.

Thalía was born in Mexico City. As a child, she sang and acted in different groups and shows. In 1990, she released her first solo album. Thalía has won many awards for her music. She is one of the most popular Mexican singers in the world.

DID YOU KNOW?

Thalía has released songs in Spanish, English, French, Portuguese, and Tagalog.

Thalía is known as the "Queen of Latin Pop."

A GREAT COUNTRY

Mexico has beautiful land and a rich history and culture. The people and places of Mexico help make the world a more interesting place.

Pico de Orizaba is the tallest mountain in Mexico. It is also North America's tallest volcano.

TOUR BOOK

If you ever visit Mexico, here are some places to go and things to do!

EXPLORE

See the Maya Pyramid of Kukulcán at Chichén Itzá.

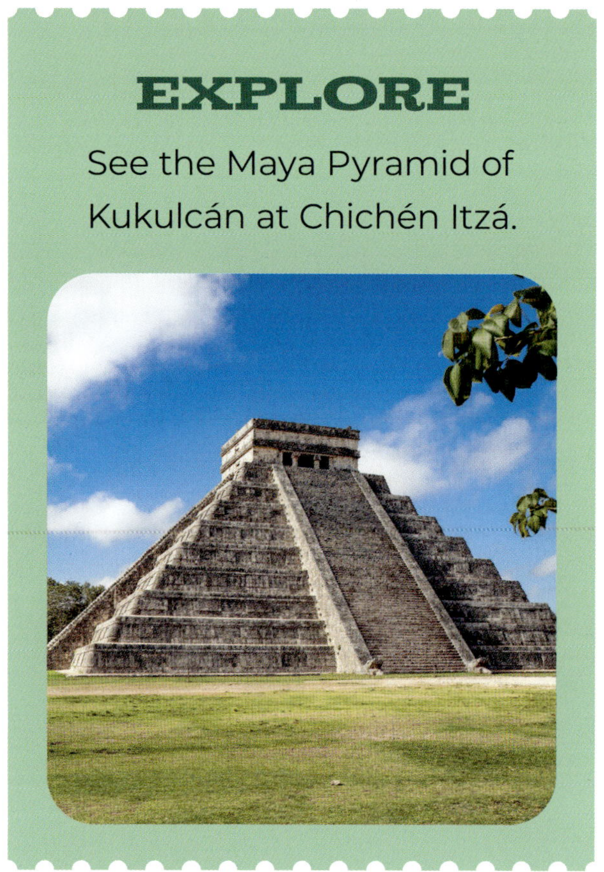

WATCH

Visit Mexico City's Bosque de Chapultepec. The park has paddleboats, gardens, a castle, and museums.

MOVE

Dance to mariachi music at the International Mariachi Festival in Guadalajara!

SEE

Hike in Chipinque Ecological Park near Monterrey. People go there to see wildlife and bike on trails.

PLAY

Build a sandcastle and play on the beautiful beaches of the Riviera Maya.

TIMELINE

ABOUT 1200 BCE

The Olmec people began building their **civilization**. It was one of the first in North America.

ABOUT 1325

The Aztecs founded Tenochtitlán. This later became Mexico City.

ABOUT 250 CE

The Maya people began to build cities and pyramids.

1521

Hernán Cortés of Spain **conquered** the Aztecs.

1810

Miguel Hidalgo y Costilla started Mexico's fight for independence.

1917

The Mexican **Revolution** officially ended with the writing of the constitution of Mexico. However, fighting continued for many more years.

2010

Mexico celebrated 200 years as an independent country.

MEXICO UP CLOSE

Official Name
Estados Unidos Mexicanos (United Mexican States)

Flag

Population
129,150,971 (2022 est.)
10th-most-populated country

Total Area
758,449 square miles (1,964,375 sq km)
14th-largest country

Official Language
Spanish

Capital
Mexico City

Currency
Mexican peso

Form of Government
Federal presidential republic

National Anthem
"Himno Nacional Mexicano" ("National Anthem of Mexico")

GLOSSARY

capital—a city where government leaders meet.

civilization—a well-organized and advanced society.

conquer (KAHN-kuhr)—to take control using military force.

federal presidential republic—a form of government in which the people choose a president to lead the country. The federal government and the individual states share power.

metropolitan area—a large city and its surrounding cities and suburbs.

natural resources—useful and valuable supplies from nature.

revolution—the forced overthrow of a government for a new system.

tradition—a belief, a custom, or a story handed down from older people to younger people.

ONLINE RESOURCES

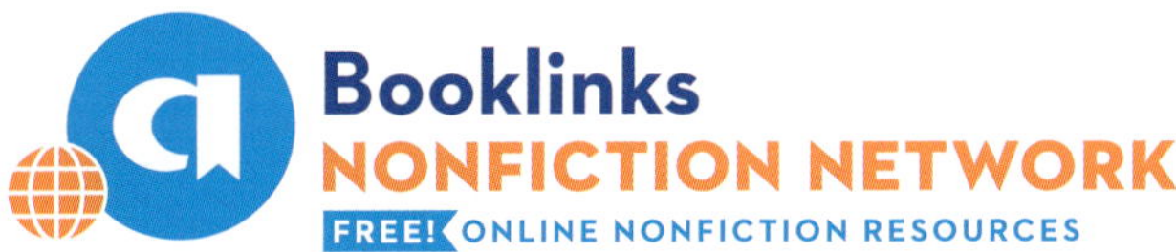

To learn more about Mexico, please visit **abdobooklinks.com** or scan this QR code. These links are routinely monitored and updated to provide the most current information available.

INDEX